COSMIC BRAIN: RETHINKING GOD, THE UNIVERSE, AND HUMAN POTENTIAL

NAVEEN KUMAR

INDIA • SINGAPORE • MALAYSIA

ISBN

Paperback 979-8-89699-478-7
Hardcase 979-8-89699-978-2

Contents

Part 4: Cosmic Brain

Part 5: Itch

Part 6: Cosmic Brain vs. God

Part 7: Law of Attraction vs. Cosmic Brain

Part 8: Desires: The Starting Point

Part 9: Effort and Energy: The Signals You Send

Part 10: Manifestation in Action

Part 11: Be Grateful for the Process

Part 12: Nazar

Part 13: Redefining Life

Part 14: Call to Action

Part 15: Exercises to Practise

Preface

For as long as I can remember, I've had a deep, unrelenting curiosity about the forces that govern our existence. Growing up in a world steeped in tradition and belief, I always found myself questioning the concept of God as presented by mainstream religions. I wondered, if God is omnipotent, omniscient, and benevolent, why does the world seem so imperfect, chaotic, and full of suffering? Why does the idea of a personal deity seem inadequate in explaining the vastness and intricacies of the universe?

This book is the culmination of that search—my quest for understanding, for clarity, and for a new perspective on what governs life. Over time, I began to explore various philosophies, religious texts, and teachings from across the world. I sought to understand how different cultures and minds tried to answer this fundamental question: What is the force that shapes and drives the universe?

Through this exploration, I arrived at an idea that has radically changed my perspective: the Cosmic Brain. This concept challenges the traditional understanding of God, not as a personal deity, but as an intelligent, interconnected system that governs everything in the universe. I believe this force is not external, but rather an intrinsic intelligence that responds to our desires, efforts, and actions—much like a brain governs the functions of a body.

In this book, I'll share with you my journey and my understanding of this force that I call the Cosmic Brain. My experiences, however subjective, have led me to this conclusion: there is something beyond our traditional understanding, a deeper intelligence that is accessible to us all, if we learn how to align with it.

I want to make it clear that this book is not written to hurt anyone's beliefs or religious sentiments. It is an exploration, a perspective—an invitation to look through a different lens. I understand that questioning long-held traditions and sacred texts can feel uncomfortable, and at times, even like a sin. But isn't that exactly what the human mind was designed for? To ask, to wonder, and to seek truth? If questioning was truly a sin, why would we have been given the capacity to do so?

So, I ask that you approach this book with an open heart and mind. This is not about rejecting anything, but about expanding our understanding of the forces at work in our lives. I believe that by examining the world through the lens of the Cosmic Brain, you may find answers, guidance, or at least a new way to look at the universe and your place in it.

Thank you for joining me on this journey of exploration. I hope that my experiences and findings resonate with you in some way, and that they help you on your own quest for meaning and understanding.

– Naveen

24/12/24

Prologue

Hypothesis: A Child's Plea to God

Before we dive into the concept of the Cosmic Brain and begin questioning the traditional definitions of God, let's consider a scenario—a hypothesis—about faith, innocence, and the nature of divine intervention.

Imagine an 8-year-old girl, a sweet and innocent child, raised to believe in the idea of a supreme being—God—who loves her, protects her, and cares for her. She has been taught from a very young age that God is her ultimate father, the ruler of the universe, and that He is always watching over her. To her, God is omnipotent (all-powerful), omniscient (all-knowing), and benevolent (all-good).

This little girl is deeply religious, carrying her faith with pure devotion. She never questions what she has been taught because, in her mind, it is a comforting truth.

One evening, as she innocently steps out to buy ice cream from the neighborhood shop, she crosses paths with an evil man. This man, driven by the darkest of intentions, kidnaps her.

When the girl realizes she is in danger, her first instinct is to call out for her parents, crying for her mother and father to come save her. But soon, she understands they cannot hear her, and in her desperation, she turns to the ultimate father—the God she has always believed in.

In her terror, she begins to pray. Her prayers are not for wealth, prosperity, or material gain. They are the purest form of prayer imaginable—a plea for her life, for safety, for a miracle.

She believes with all her heart that God, being omnipotent, can save her because He is all-powerful.

She believes that God, being omniscient, knows exactly where she is and what is happening to her.

And she believes that God, being benevolent, would never allow harm to befall an innocent child.

Her faith is unshaken as she cries out, "Please save me, God."

Now, I ask you: **What would God do?**

If God is truly the way He has been defined for centuries—omnipotent, omniscient, and benevolent—then saving this child is not just a possibility; it is an obligation of His divine nature. This act would require no effort, no struggle, and no compromise, for such a God can do anything.

Yet, we know what happens next.

The reality of our world is painfully clear. We have seen countless stories like this one, through the news and in our lives, where innocent children suffer unimaginable horrors. These are not isolated incidents but a recurring and undeniable truth of our existence.

So, the question arises:

If God exists as traditionally defined, where is He in moments like these? Why does He allow such suffering? Does the God we've been taught to believe in really govern this world? Or is it time to reconsider what we mean by 'God'?

This book is not about questioning faith but about seeking answers. It is about moving beyond comforting beliefs to discover the true governing force of this universe—one that explains the reality we live in and empowers us to shape our lives in meaningful ways.

Acknowledgements

This is my first book, and to be honest, I never intended to become an author, especially on a subject as deeply personal and thought-provoking as this one. However, as I continuously questioned the world around me and shared my insights with those closest to me, it became clear that I had something valuable to share. These conversations sparked the realization that my philosophy might resonate with others, leading me to write this book.

I am deeply grateful to my father, whose wisdom and encouragement allowed me to explore life on my own terms, even in the face of a traditional society's expectations. His belief in my independence and judgment has shaped me profoundly and continues to be a source of strength.

This book is a testament to the influence, support, and love I've received from everyone who has been part of this journey. I hope this work reflects the impact you've had on my life and does justice to everything you've done for me.

Thank you, from the depths of my heart.

The Traditional Definition of God and Its Flaws

The Traditional Definition of God and Its Flaws

Throughout history, God has often been defined as an omnipotent (all-powerful), omniscient (all-knowing), and benevolent (perfectly good) entity. This portrayal presents God as a divine being who governs the universe with perfect knowledge, power, and compassion. While this idea has offered solace to many, it becomes increasingly difficult to reconcile with the harsh realities of life.

If such a being truly existed, one might expect the world to be free from suffering, chaos, and injustice—a harmonious realm where good prevails and evil is eradicated. However, our lived reality tells a different story:

1. **Suffering and Tragedy**

   Innocent people face unimaginable hardships—wars ravage nations, diseases claim millions of lives, and natural disasters destroy entire communities. For example, why would an all-powerful and benevolent God allow innocent children to die from famine or devastating illnesses?

2. **Flourishing of Evil**

   Throughout history, we've seen individuals commit heinous acts and often escape accountability. If God is all-knowing, wouldn't He foresee such actions? If He is all-powerful, why wouldn't He intervene to prevent them?

3. **Inequality and Injustice**

   The world is rife with systemic inequalities—wealth and resources are distributed unevenly, and justice is often denied to those who need it most. Why would a benevolent God permit such disparities to persist?

These contradictions compel us to ask profound questions:

- If God is all-knowing, does He not see this suffering?
- If God is all-powerful, does He not have the ability to stop it?
- And if God is benevolent, why does He allow it to persist?

Traditional definitions of God fail to provide satisfactory answers to these questions, leaving a void that challenges the validity of these long-held views.

The Limitations of Traditional Beliefs

Religious teachings often respond to these contradictions by introducing concepts like free will, divine tests, or mysterious plans beyond human comprehension. However, these explanations often fall short in addressing the scale and intensity of human and natural suffering.

- **Free Will Argument**: While free will might explain human actions, it doesn't account for natural disasters or diseases, which are beyond human control.

- **Divine Test Argument**: If suffering is a test, why are some individuals subjected to immeasurable pain while others lead relatively charmed lives?
- **Mystery Argument**: Claiming that God's ways are beyond human understanding provides no tangible comfort or resolution to those enduring hardships.

These justifications often seem like attempts to rationalize an inherently flawed model of divinity rather than addressing the root contradictions.

A Shift in Perspective

Rather than clinging to a definition of God that fails to align with observable reality, we might consider alternative frameworks that make sense of the universe as it is. The concept of the Cosmic Brain, for example, reframes the governing force of the universe as impartial and responsive, rather than omnipotent or benevolent. It operates based on laws and signals, not moral judgments or selective intervention.

This shift in perspective offers a rational, actionable understanding of life's challenges and opportunities without relying on outdated and often contradictory notions of divinity. By stepping away from the limitations of traditional definitions, we open ourselves to a deeper exploration of existence—one that aligns with both logic and experience.

Philosophies Through the Ages

Philosophies Through the Ages: Understanding the Evolution of God Concepts

Throughout human history, the concept of God has been shaped by the cultural, intellectual, and environmental contexts of different civilizations. These interpretations have evolved over time, influenced by the knowledge and imagination available during each era. By examining how these ideas must have emerged, we can gain insight into the human need to explain the universe, find purpose, and seek a governing force in their lives.

1. The Earliest Notions: Animism and Nature Worship

Era: Prehistoric and early tribal societies.

Philosophy: God as the embodiment of nature.

In the earliest human societies, people lived closely with nature. They depended on the seasons, animals, rivers, and forests for survival. Lacking scientific understanding, they personified natural forces as gods and spirits.

- **Sun and Moon Worship**: The sun was seen as a giver of life, while the moon influenced tides and cycles.

- **Rain and Thunder Gods**: Rain was critical for crops, and thunder was awe-inspiring, leading to gods like Indra in Hinduism or Thor in Norse mythology.
- **Animal Spirits**: Animals that played crucial roles in survival, such as the buffalo or eagle, were revered as divine beings or totems.

The emergence of these beliefs was rooted in gratitude and fear. Early humans sought to appease these gods through rituals, offerings, and dances, hoping to gain favor or avoid calamity.

2. Polytheism: Gods for Every Aspect of Life

Era: Early civilizations (Mesopotamia, Egypt, Greece, India).

Philosophy: A pantheon of gods governing different realms.

As societies became more structured, their understanding of divinity expanded into systems of polytheism. In these civilizations, gods were given specific roles, powers, and personalities, often mirroring human traits:

- **Mesopotamia:** Gods like Enlil (storm and wind) and Ishtar (love and war) reflected the unpredictable and dual nature of life.
- **Egypt:** Deities like Ra (the sun god) and Osiris (god of the afterlife) helped explain natural phenomena and the mystery of death.
- **Greece:** Philosophers and poets like Homer anthropomorphized gods such as Zeus, Hera, and Athena, creating relatable, flawed deities.
- **India:** The Vedic period gave rise to a rich pantheon of gods, each representing natural and cosmic forces. For instance, Agni (the fire god) symbolized transformation and was central to rituals, while Indra (the king of gods) was associated with rain and storms, reflecting his importance in an agrarian society.

The organization of gods into pantheons likely started from the hierarchical structures of early cities. Just as kings and rulers governed people, gods governed aspects of the world. Temples and priesthoods became central to maintaining these divine-human relationships, offering a way to honor these deities and seek their favor in daily life.

3. The Rise of Monotheism: A Singular Supreme Being

Era: Around 2000 BCE to 500 CE (Abrahamic religions, Zoroastrianism).

Philosophy: One God above all creation.

As societies grew larger and more interconnected, the idea of a singular, all-powerful deity gained prominence:

- **Judaism:** The idea of Yahweh as the one true God emerged among the ancient Hebrews, emphasizing covenant, morality, and justice.
- **Zoroastrianism:** In Persia, Zoroaster introduced Ahura Mazda, a singular god representing good, opposed by Angra Mainyu, the force of evil. This dualistic worldview influenced later monotheistic traditions.
- **Christianity and Islam:** These faiths built upon earlier monotheistic ideas, portraying God as both transcendent and personal, capable of love and mercy but also justice and wrath.

Monotheism often emerged in response to the complexities of polytheistic systems. A single, universal God provided unity and simplicity, especially for expanding empires and societies seeking common ground.

4. Philosophical and Abstract Concepts of God

Era: Classical Antiquity (Greek, Indian, and Chinese philosophies).

Philosophy: God as an abstract principle or universal truth.

With the rise of intellectual traditions, thinkers began to explore more philosophical and less anthropomorphic ideas of God:

- **Greek Philosophy**: Philosophers like Plato and Aristotle viewed God not as a personal being but as an eternal, perfect entity.

Aristotle's "Unmoved Mover" was a rational force that set the universe in motion without direct involvement.

- **Indian Philosophy:** In the Upanishads, Brahman (Para Brahman) was described as the ultimate, formless reality underlying all existence. Unlike personal deities, Brahman was beyond human comprehension, a concept that formed the foundation of Hindu philosophy.

- **Chinese Philosophy:** Confucianism and Taoism emphasized harmony with the cosmos. Tao (The Way) was an impersonal force guiding the natural order, contrasting with the idea of a personal god.

These abstract concepts arose in societies with advanced education and philosophical traditions. They represented a shift from myth to reason, offering a way to reconcile spirituality with intellectual inquiry.

5. The Role of Fear and Power in Shaping God Concepts

Throughout these eras, the idea of God was often used as a tool to maintain order and power. Rulers and priests claimed divine authority to enforce laws, control populations, and justify wars. The fear of divine punishment was a powerful motivator for compliance.

- **Kings as Gods:** Egyptian pharaohs were considered gods on Earth, bridging the human and divine realms.

- **Divine Mandates:** In China, the "Mandate of Heaven" justified the rule of emperors, asserting that their power was granted by a higher force.

- **Fear of Hell and Wrath**: Many religious systems introduced concepts of punishment in the afterlife to ensure adherence to moral codes.

6. The Transition to Modernity: Questioning Traditional Concepts

Era: The Enlightenment to present day.

Philosophy: God as a metaphor or irrelevant to the universe.

With advancements in science and technology, humanity began to find natural explanations for phenomena once attributed to gods:

- **Scientific Revolutions**: Discoveries in astronomy, biology, and physics demystified the cosmos, challenging the literal interpretations of religious texts.
- **Philosophical Atheism:** Thinkers like Nietzsche declared "God is dead," reflecting the diminishing role of traditional religion in a rational, secular world.
- **Spirituality without Religion:** In modern times, many people view God not as a being but as a metaphor for universal energy, consciousness, or interconnectedness.

While these philosophies provided valuable frameworks for their time, they were ultimately limited by humanity's knowledge and understanding. Many of these ideas were tailored to the specific fears and needs of the societies that created them, resulting in fragmented and sometimes contradictory depictions of divinity and universal governance.

The Inaccuracies in Religious Philosophies

As humanity has progressed, the traditional philosophies underpinning religion often fail to align with our contemporary understanding of the world. Science, reason, and modern sensibilities have exposed the limitations of many age-old religious doctrines.

Key Issues:

1. **Outdated Texts**:
    - Religious texts, written centuries ago, reflect the cultural and scientific knowledge of their time. While some teachings

remain timeless, many have become obsolete or irrelevant in today's context.

2. **Ritualistic Practices**:
   - Rituals that once held symbolic or practical significance are now viewed as superstitions or meaningless traditions by many. These practices often lack connection to the challenges and aspirations of modern life.

3. **The Personal God Fallacy**:
   - The idea of a personal, interventionist God who answers prayers, rewards virtue, and punishes wrongdoing is increasingly at odds with observable reality. Many people find their prayers unanswered and injustices unaddressed, leading to disillusionment.

Religious philosophies often simplify or mystify the complexities of existence, leaving critical questions about the universe, consciousness, and the governing force unanswered. As a result, many individuals today are disillusioned with traditional religious frameworks and yearn for a perspective that resonates with their lived experiences.

Conclusion

The concept of God has always reflected humanity's need to understand and navigate the mysteries of existence. From nature worship to monotheism, and from philosophical abstraction to modern skepticism, these ideas have evolved with our knowledge and experiences.

As we journey through this book, we'll explore how these fragmented philosophies can be reconciled in the idea of the **Cosmic Brain**—a universal force that aligns with modern understanding while addressing the eternal questions that have driven humanity for millennia.

Religious Rituals and Their Obsolescence

Religious Rituals and Their Obsolescence

Religious rituals have historically played a significant role in shaping human societies. They were created to foster community, provide a sense of order, and connect individuals with the divine or the supernatural. However, as societies have evolved, many of these rituals have lost their relevance, meaning, or practicality in the modern world. While some rituals may still hold cultural or emotional significance, others seem disconnected from reality and offer little in terms of actionable, results-driven approaches to life.

1. Rituals Rooted in Superstition

Example: Breaking a coconut to remove obstacles.

In many cultures, breaking a coconut in front of a deity is seen as a way to remove obstacles in life. While the act has symbolic significance—representing the breaking of the ego or a fresh start—it does not directly contribute to solving problems or overcoming challenges.

- **Gap**: A person facing financial difficulties or a career setback is unlikely to find practical solutions through this ritual alone. Actionable steps such as skill-building, networking, or financial planning are required.

Obsolescence: These rituals may comfort individuals or provide a psychological placebo, but they do not address the root causes of life's challenges in a tangible way.

2. Fasting for Divine Favor
Example: Observing fasts for blessings, such as during Ramadan, Navratri, or Lent.

Fasting is often performed with the belief that it brings divine blessings, forgiveness, or spiritual merit. While fasting can have health benefits when done properly, the intended religious outcomes—such as gaining favor from God—lack empirical evidence.

- **Gap**: The person fasting for financial prosperity or family well-being would be better served by actively working toward those goals rather than relying solely on divine intervention.

Obsolescence: In a world where measurable effort and strategic planning yield results, fasting as a means of achieving practical goals seems outdated.

3. Animal Sacrifices
Example: Offering animals to appease gods or ancestors.

In some cultures, animals are sacrificed during religious ceremonies to gain favor, ward off evil, or ensure a good harvest. While these practices may have had cultural or spiritual importance in ancient times, they often appear cruel and unnecessary today.

- **Gap**: Modern agricultural techniques, weather prediction technologies, and sustainable farming practices can ensure better harvests without resorting to such rituals.

Obsolescence: The practice is not only inhumane but also fails to align with contemporary ethical and environmental standards.

4. Pilgrimages as a Means to Purge Sin
Example: Walking hundreds of miles or bathing in sacred rivers to cleanse one's sins.

Many religions encourage pilgrimages to holy sites as a way to gain spiritual merit or wash away sins. For instance, the Ganges River in India is believed to purify the soul, and the Hajj in Islam is a journey of immense spiritual significance.

- **Gap**: While these acts may offer emotional and spiritual fulfillment, they do not address the consequences of one's actions or promote personal growth. A person who has committed wrongs may gain more by making amends, engaging in self-reflection, or working on self-improvement.

Obsolescence: The idea that physical acts can erase moral or ethical failings oversimplifies the complexity of human behavior and responsibility.

5. Lighting Lamps or Incense for Wealth and Prosperity

Example: Performing aarti (lamp offering) or lighting incense to invite wealth into the home.

In many households, rituals involving the lighting of lamps, burning incense, or placing specific symbols are believed to attract prosperity and drive away misfortune.

- **Gap**: Wealth and success are better achieved through education, hard work, and strategic financial planning, not through symbolic acts.

Obsolescence: While such rituals may create a positive atmosphere, they do little to directly influence economic outcomes.

6. Astrology-Based Rituals

Example: Wearing gemstones, performing poojas, or conducting ceremonies to nullify the effects of planetary alignments.

Astrology often dictates rituals to mitigate the supposed negative effects of celestial bodies on one's life. This includes wearing gemstones for luck, conducting ceremonies to appease planets, or postponing significant events based on "inauspicious" timings.

- **Gap**: These practices are based on pseudoscience and ignore the actual factors affecting success or failure, such as preparation, timing, and execution.

Obsolescence: Modern astronomy has debunked many astrological claims, making such rituals scientifically untenable.

7. Ritualistic Charity for Religious Merit
Example: Donating money or food to temples in exchange for blessings.

Many believe that giving to religious institutions guarantees divine favor or improves their karma. While charity is a noble act, doing it for spiritual points reduces its sincerity and potential impact.

- **Gap**: Donating directly to organizations addressing societal issues—such as education, healthcare, or poverty alleviation—has a far more measurable and meaningful effect.

Obsolescence: Ritualistic charity often prioritizes religious institutions over addressing real-world problems.

Bridging the Gap

Modern challenges demand practical, results-oriented approaches, yet faith-based rituals continue to dominate in many communities. This disconnect arises because:

1. **Comfort Zone**: Rituals provide emotional security and a sense of control in uncertain situations.
2. **Cultural Inertia**: Many rituals are deeply ingrained in traditions and are difficult to abandon, even when they no longer serve a purpose.
3. **Lack of Awareness**: Many people are unaware of alternative, actionable solutions to their problems.

Conclusion

Religious rituals have served their purpose in history, often reflecting the knowledge and needs of their time. However, as humanity progresses, clinging to outdated practices can hinder growth and prevent individuals from addressing real-world problems effectively.

The concept of the **Cosmic Brain** challenges this approach, advocating for a reality-driven philosophy where tangible efforts, focused thoughts, and intentional actions replace blind faith in rituals. By aligning our actions with universal principles of energy and manifestation, we can bridge the gap between spiritual aspirations and practical results, creating a more empowered and meaningful life.

Cosmic Brain

What is the Cosmic Brain?

The Cosmic Brain is a revolutionary concept that seeks to redefine the way we perceive the governing force of the universe. It is not a deity, not a supernatural being sitting on a throne in the heavens, but rather an interconnected, universal intelligence that operates as a byproduct of the universe itself. It is akin to human consciousness, which emerges from the brain—a physical body—yet functions as the guiding force of our actions and thoughts. The Cosmic Brain represents a new perspective on how the universe works, rooted in observable phenomena and rational thought.

Understanding the Universe and Its Consciousness

One undeniable truth of the universe is our own existence as conscious beings. We, as humans, possess awareness and the ability to comprehend our surroundings. Through modern science, we have not only identified what we can see with the naked eye but also uncovered countless phenomena invisible to us, from electromagnetic fields to distant galaxies. This exploration has revealed the incredible complexity of the universe, challenging us to ask deeper questions about its governing principles.

The universe is composed of two categories:

1. **Tangible Entities:** Physical forms like rocks, rivers, mountains, celestial bodies, and living organisms.
2. **Intangible Phenomena:** Abstract forces like gravity, inertia, electromagnetic fields, emotions, and consciousness, which emerge from or are associated with physical entities.

Science has shown us that intangible phenomena do not exist independently—they are always tied to the tangible. For example:

- **Emotions and feelings** are byproducts of the brain and nervous system.
- **Electromagnetic fields** emanate from objects with electromagnetic properties.
- **Gravity** exists due to the presence of mass.

Thus, if there is a governing force in the universe—a superconsciousness or intelligence—it must either have a tangible form or be a byproduct of something tangible.

Why Traditional Definitions of God Fall Short

The traditional idea of a god with a physical form, governing the universe yet hidden from empirical discovery, seems increasingly implausible in the face of modern science. We have explored the cosmos through advanced technologies, probing the edges of the observable universe, yet there is no evidence of a divine figure orchestrating everything.

This raises an important question: Could the governing force of the universe be a byproduct of the universe itself, rather than an external entity?

Introducing the Cosmic Brain

The Cosmic Brain is the byproduct of the universe, much like human consciousness is the byproduct of the brain. Just as our brain governs every action and process in our body, the Cosmic Brain governs the universe's functioning, from the movements of celestial bodies to the evolution of life and the flow of rivers.

To understand this better, let's draw a parallel between the human body and the universe:

1. **The Human Body:**
    - Our brain acts as the control center. It governs voluntary actions like eating and walking, as well as involuntary processes like digestion and heartbeat.
    - When one part of the body signals a need—like the stomach feeling hungry—the brain responds by coordinating actions to fulfill that need.
2. **The Universe:**
    - The Cosmic Brain acts as the universe's control center, though it is not a physical organ. It is an emergent intelligence, arising from the interconnectedness of all things in existence.
    - It governs the flow of energy, the dynamics of celestial bodies, and even the unfolding of human innovations and ideas.

The Role of the Cosmic Brain in Manifestation

Much like our human brain responds to the needs and signals from the body, the Cosmic Brain responds to the needs and intentions of the universe, including human desires. For instance:

- When you intensely desire something and take action toward it, this process sends signals to the Cosmic Brain.
- The Cosmic Brain, operating through the laws of energy and causation, creates opportunities and pathways for your desires to manifest, much like the brain mobilizes the body to satisfy hunger or respond to danger.

This principle also explains the autonomous nature of certain phenomena:

- The solar system functions with precision, following gravitational laws, as if guided by a larger intelligence.
- Rivers flow to their natural destinations, carving landscapes along the way.
- Hum**an innovations** emerge from a collective consciousness, inspired by a universal intelligence.

Why the Cosmic Brain Makes Sense

The Cosmic Brain is a unifying concept that bridges the gap between science and spirituality:

1. **Emergence from Tangibility:**

   It arises naturally from the universe's physical and energetic components, much like consciousness arises from the brain.

2. **Explains Autonomy:**

   It accounts for the autonomous functioning of universal phenomena, from the orbits of planets to the behavior of ecosystems.

3. **Empowers Individuals:**

   Unlike traditional religious beliefs that rely on an external deity for intervention, the Cosmic Brain empowers individuals to take intentional actions that align with universal principles, thereby influencing their reality.

What the Cosmic Brain is Not

- **Not a Supernatural Entity:** The Cosmic Brain is not an external god controlling the universe from afar.
- Not a Physical Organ: Unlike the human brain, the Cosmic Brain has no specific physical form. It is an emergent property of the interconnected universe.
- Not Bound **by Faith:** Its existence and principles do not depend on belief but can be understood through observation and logic.

Conclusion: The Cosmic Brain as the Universe's Intelligence

The Cosmic Brain represents a paradigm shift in understanding the universe. By viewing the universe as an interconnected whole, governed by a collective intelligence, we move away from outdated notions of divine intervention and embrace a model rooted in reality and empowerment.

In upcoming chapters, we will explore how the Cosmic Brain works, how it interacts with human consciousness, and how we can align our desires and actions with its principles to manifest our goals and live meaningful lives.

Itch

The Itch Principle: Turning Desire into Destiny

Life's challenges and goals often seem overwhelming or unattainable. However, understanding the process of how things work in the broader context of the universe can provide a roadmap for achieving anything we desire. A simple yet powerful analogy to illustrate this is the phenomenon of Itch. Let's delve into how this everyday experience mirrors the workings of the Cosmic Brain and can guide us toward achieving our dreams.

The Science of Itching

When we feel an itch, it is essentially a chemical reaction triggered by an irritant or foreign substance on the skin. This reaction activates the skin cells, which then send signals to the brain to indicate discomfort. The brain evaluates these signals, determines their intensity, and sends a command to the hand (or another tool) to scratch the affected area. This process alleviates the irritation, offering relief.

However, there are key observations within this mechanism:

1. **Intensity Matters:**

    - If the itch is mild, the brain may not act immediately, or we might ignore it altogether.

- If the itch is intense, it demands attention, compelling the brain to take immediate action.

2. **Creative Problem-Solving:**

    - When the itch is on an inaccessible part of the body, like the back, and the hand cannot reach it, the brain finds alternatives—using a stick, a wall, or even asking someone for help.

These elements—**stimulus, intensity, action, and problem-solving**—are not just limited to the biology of itching. They reflect universal principles that apply to achieving goals in life.

The Cosmic Brain and the Itch Analogy

In the grander scheme, each of us can be seen as a cell within the body of the universe, and the Cosmic Brain is its governing intelligence. Just as the cells in our body signal the human brain to address their needs, we send signals to the Cosmic Brain through our desires, thoughts, and actions.

Here's how this works:

1. Initiating the Signal: The First Step

When a cell in your body reacts to a foreign substance, it initiates the process of sending a signal to the brain. Similarly, in life, the first step to achieving a goal is to form a clear desire. This desire is like the chemical reaction—it triggers the need and sends the initial signal to the Cosmic Brain.

However, desire alone is not enough. The signal becomes stronger when you take action, no matter how small. This could be researching, learning, or making incremental progress toward your goal. The key is to start. Just as the itch begins with a reaction, your journey begins with a decision and a step forward.

2. Consistent Effort: Strengthening the Signal

The intensity of an itch determines how urgently the brain responds. If the sensation is mild, it might go unnoticed or be ignored. But if it's persistent and intense, the brain prioritizes it, mobilizing resources to find relief.

Likewise, in life, achieving goals requires consistent and focused effort. By repeatedly sending signals to the Cosmic Brain—through persistent action, thinking about your goal, and reinforcing your desire—you increase the intensity of the "itch." This compels the Cosmic Brain to take action on your behalf.

If your effort is sporadic or your desire weak, the Cosmic Brain may treat it as faint noise, much like the brain might ignore a mild itch. Consistency is key to ensuring your goal receives attention.

3. Trust the Cosmic Brain to Find a Way

When the itch is on an inaccessible part of the body, the human brain finds creative solutions, like using a stick to scratch the back. Similarly, the Cosmic Brain has its own ways of solving problems and aligning circumstances to help you achieve your goal.

Even if your goal seems impossible or you have no idea how to accomplish it, that's not your concern. Your job is to consistently desire and work toward the goal. The Cosmic Brain will handle the "how," aligning opportunities, resources, and people in ways you might not expect.

The universe, like the body, operates on a feedback loop. When you consistently send clear, intense signals, the Cosmic Brain responds, finding a path—even in the face of obstacles.

The Dangers of Faint Signals

If you desire something but fail to take consistent action, the Cosmic Brain may treat your signal as weak and ignore it. This is akin to a mild itch that doesn't compel you to scratch. Weak signals fail to generate urgency or response.

Think of all the times you've wished for something but didn't put in the effort or belief to back it up. Such faint signals rarely produce results because they lack intensity and persistence.

The Takeaway: Manifestation Through Action and Belief

The analogy of Itch teaches us profound truths about life:

1. **Desire is the starting point.** It triggers the initial signal to the Cosmic Brain.
2. **Action amplifies the signal.** Each step, no matter how small, strengthens your intent.
3. **Consistency is critical.** Persistent effort ensures your goal remains a priority for the Cosmic Brain.
4. **Trust the process.** The Cosmic Brain will find ways to align the universe to meet your needs, just as the human brain mobilizes resources to scratch an itch.

By understanding and applying these principles, you can align yourself with the workings of the Cosmic Brain and achieve what may seem impossible. Whether it's a personal goal, a professional ambition, or a lifelong dream, the process remains the same: desire, act, persist, and trust. The universe will do the rest.

Cosmic Brain vs. God

How the Cosmic Brain Differs from Traditional God: Practicality Over Faith

Throughout history, the concept of God has served as a foundation for creating morals, ethics, and laws. Ancient societies relied on the belief in a divine being to establish frameworks for peace, harmony, and survival. These religious morals often reflected the natural human need for cooperation and order, which are essential for thriving as a community. However, as societies have evolved, it has become evident that these systems are no longer dependent on faith or divine intervention. Let's explore how the Cosmic Brain differs from the traditional idea of God, emphasizing practicality and natural laws over faith-based beliefs.

1. Morals and Ethics: From Religion to Law

Religious teachings historically served as a moral compass, offering guidelines for right and wrong. While many of these values—such as kindness, honesty, and justice—are crucial for peaceful coexistence, they are not exclusive to religion. Over time, societies have codified these principles into laws and constitutions, which serve the same purpose without invoking the fear of divine punishment or hell.

For example:

- Religious texts may dictate "Thou shalt not kill," backed by the fear of eternal damnation.
- Modern constitutions uphold the same value through laws that punish murder with imprisonment or other legal consequences.

The shift from faith-based morality to secular governance highlights a critical difference: **we no longer need religion to regulate behavior.** The fear of jail, rather than hell, now ensures accountability in most societies.

While many religious values have been foundational in building moral and ethical systems, not all of them serve humanity's best interests in the modern world. Over time, some religious teachings have been used to justify control over specific genders, communities, and behaviors, often perpetuating inequality, prejudice, and division. These outdated moral codes clash with the impartial and universal laws of nature, which apply equally to all beings.

Gender Inequality in Religious Teachings

Many religions, particularly those formed in patriarchal societies, have historically placed men in dominant roles while relegating women to subservient or secondary positions.

- **Example: Restriction on Leadership Roles**
    - In several religious traditions, women are barred from becoming priests, imams, or other spiritual leaders. For example, in Roman Catholicism, women cannot be ordained as priests, despite their equal intellectual and spiritual capabilities.
    - This restriction reflects an outdated worldview rather than any inherent difference in ability.

- **Example: Dress Codes for Women**
    - Some religious teachings impose strict dress codes on women, such as requiring them to wear veils or cover their entire bodies. While often justified as a sign of modesty, these rules frequently stem from a desire to control women's autonomy and choices.
    - The law of nature, in contrast, does not distinguish between genders in terms of their inherent rights or abilities. Gravity pulls a woman to the ground with the same force it does a man; the universe recognizes no hierarchy based on gender.

Caste and Class Discrimination

Religious doctrines have also been used to enforce rigid social hierarchies, often resulting in the systemic oppression of certain groups.

- **Example: The Caste System in Hinduism**
    - The caste system, deeply rooted in ancient religious texts, categorizes people into hierarchical groups based on birth. Those in "lower castes" have historically been denied access to education, opportunities, and basic human rights.
    - While many societies have legally abolished caste-based discrimination, its remnants persist, creating inequality and prejudice.
    - In contrast, nature does not assign a higher value to one individual over another. A natural disaster like an earthquake does not spare someone because of their caste; it treats everyone equally.

Religious Justifications for Slavery

In the past, many religious texts were used to justify the practice of slavery.

- **Example: Biblical Endorsements of Slavery**
    - Certain passages in the Bible were interpreted to support slavery, such as instructions for slaves to obey their masters (e.g., Ephesians 6:5).
    - This religious justification allowed the exploitation of millions of people over centuries, often under the guise of divine approval.
    - The law of nature, however, does not discriminate based on social status or power dynamics. All humans require the same basic elements for survival, such as air, water, and food, regardless of their societal roles.

Discrimination Based on Sexual Orientation

Religious teachings have frequently been used to marginalize individuals based on their sexual orientation.

- **Example: Condemnation of Homosexuality**
    - Many religious doctrines label homosexuality as a sin, leading to widespread discrimination and exclusion of LGBTQ+ individuals.
    - This has caused immense psychological harm and perpetuated societal stigma, even though scientific evidence shows that sexual orientation is a natural variation in human behavior.
    - Natural laws, on the other hand, do not differentiate between individuals based on who they love. The same principles of physics, biology, and chemistry apply to everyone equally.

Suppression of Scientific Progress

Religious dogma has often been used to suppress scientific discoveries and intellectual advancement.

- **Example: The Persecution of Galileo**
    - In the 17th century, Galileo was tried by the Catholic Church for supporting the heliocentric model of the solar system, which contradicted religious teachings at the time.
    - This suppression of scientific progress slowed humanity's understanding of the universe, even though natural laws like gravity and planetary motion remained constant, indifferent to human beliefs.

Imposed Behavioral Restrictions

Religious teachings often impose behavioral restrictions that may have once had practical reasons but are now obsolete.

- **Example: Dietary Laws**
    - Many religions prohibit specific foods, such as pork in Islam and Judaism or beef in Hinduism. While these restrictions may have originated from health concerns or cultural preferences, they are often presented as divine mandates.
    - Today, with advancements in hygiene and food safety, such prohibitions are no longer universally relevant.

The Fear-Based Control of Communities

Many religious systems maintain control over followers by instilling fear of divine punishment or eternal damnation.

- **Example: Fear of Hell**
    - Religions often use the concept of hell to deter people from breaking moral codes, even when those codes are arbitrary or oppressive.
    - This fear-based approach can stifle free thought, creativity, and personal growth, which are essential for human progress.
    - Nature, in contrast, does not punish or reward; it simply exists. A plant grows when given sunlight and water, regardless of whether it is in the garden of a believer or a skeptic.

2. Nature's Laws: Impartial and Unyielding

The laws of nature, unlike religious teachings, do not discriminate based on morality, intention, or belief. They apply equally to everyone—saint or sinner, believer or atheist.

Take this scenario:

- A saint and a criminal are in a car that falls from a broken bridge. Does gravity consider the moral character of the individuals? No. Both fall at the same rate, governed by the same natural law.

This impartiality of natural laws demonstrates their inherent fairness. The universe doesn't reward or punish based on human-made concepts of good and evil. It simply follows its own principles.

The **Cosmic Brain**, much like natural laws, operates on principles that transcend morality. It does not differentiate between a criminal's intent to harm and a saint's desire to help. Instead, it responds to the **intensity** of desire and the **consistency** of effort.

3. Cosmic Brain: Driven by Intensity, Not Intention

The Cosmic Brain is not a benevolent deity judging the morality of your desires. It is a universal intelligence that operates on energy and manifestation. Its primary mechanism is the **intensity** of your desire and the **actions** you take to fulfill it.

This is why people with bad intentions—such as criminals—do achieve their goals. Their intense focus and relentless efforts send strong signals to the Cosmic Brain, which responds without bias. For example:

- A person with malicious intent, like committing a crime, may succeed because they are singularly focused on their goal.
- Similarly, an inventor or artist, fueled by passion, achieves greatness through the same mechanism: intensity and consistent effort.

This impartiality may seem unsettling at first, but it also highlights a profound truth: **we have the power to shape the world we want.**

4. Overcoming Evil Through Collective Desires

The impartial nature of the Cosmic Brain does not mean evil will always triumph. While individuals with bad intentions may succeed temporarily, the collective desire for peace, harmony, and progress holds greater weight.

The Cosmic Brain prioritizes the strongest and most consistent signals. If humanity as a whole channels its energy into desiring a better world—one free from violence, inequality, and suffering—the Cosmic Brain will respond to that.

Here's how this works:

- When millions of people work toward a common goal, such as environmental sustainability or global peace, their collective efforts and intensity amplify the signal to the Cosmic Brain.
- This unified desire creates opportunities, solutions, and innovations that align with the collective vision, outpacing individual efforts with harmful intentions.

Thus, instead of worrying about those who misuse the Cosmic Brain's principles, we should focus on strengthening our collective desire for good.

5. Practicality Over Faith

Unlike traditional concepts of God, which rely on faith, rituals, and morality, the Cosmic Brain emphasizes **practicality**:

- **It does not require belief or worship.** You don't have to pray or follow rituals to activate the Cosmic Brain; you only need to act with intensity and consistency.
- **It operates on universal principles, not morality.** The Cosmic Brain is neither good nor evil. It simply responds to the energy and effort you put into your desires.
- **It empowers rather than judges.** The Cosmic Brain doesn't punish or reward based on arbitrary rules. Instead, it gives everyone the tools to manifest their reality through action and persistence.

Conclusion: A Better World Through Understanding

The Cosmic Brain represents a shift from faith-based systems to a more practical and empowering understanding of the universe. By recognizing that the Cosmic Brain responds to intensity rather than intention, we can focus on what truly matters:

- Desiring and working toward a better world.
- Aligning our individual goals with collective progress.
- Taking consistent action to manifest our dreams.

When we channel our collective energy into positive outcomes, the Cosmic Brain responds. It doesn't judge us for who we are or what we believe. Instead, it reflects the energy we put out into the universe, giving us the power to shape our reality.

Law of Attraction vs. Cosmic Brain

Cosmic Brain vs. Law of Attraction

The **Law of Attraction** suggests that to achieve something, you need to manifest your desires by visualizing and believing in them. It emphasizes three steps:

1. **Ask** – Identify what you want.
2. **Believe** – Trust that it's already coming to you.
3. **Receive** – Be ready to accept it when it arrives.

While this concept has inspired many and is often credited by successful people, it overlooks a critical component: **action**. The belief that you can simply "think" your way to success disregards the steps and effort required to activate the process.

The **Cosmic Brain**, on the other hand, insists that desire and belief are just the starting points. What truly triggers results is the combination of **consistent action**, **clear intention**, and **gratitude**—elements that ensure the universe (or Cosmic Brain) takes notice and responds.

How the Cosmic Brain Differs

The **Cosmic Brain** model argues that manifestation is only one part of a larger equation. Merely believing and asking is insufficient; what activates the Cosmic Brain's response is **consistent effort and intentional focus.** Here's how it works:

1. **Desire (The Catalyst)**
    - Every achievement begins with **desire**. This could be inspired by internal longings, external influences, or seemingly impossible dreams.
    - Desire is akin to the first itch, triggered by an external stimulus (like a chemical reaction on your skin). Similarly, your desire acts as the initial "signal" to the Cosmic Brain.
    - **Key Insight:** Don't limit your desires by doubting their feasibility. Wealth, health, relationships, or recognition—no matter how grand your dreams seem, every desire starts the process.
2. **Take the First Step (Activate the Signal)**
    - The Law of Attraction often misses this critical step. Simply "asking" does not send a strong enough signal to the Cosmic Brain. You must act.
    - Even if you don't know the how, start with the smallest step: research, brainstorm, or try something new. This action serves as the initial chemical reaction of your metaphorical "itch." It begins the signaling process to the Cosmic Brain.
    - Example: If you want to write a book, start by writing a single sentence or brainstorming ideas. The signal strengthens as you move forward.

3. **Consistency in Action and Belief**

    - Action alone won't suffice. You must **pair consistent work with unwaver**ing belief in your ultimate goal.
    - This is where many lose focus. If you act without belief or clarity, you might achieve smaller, disconnected goals but fail to align with your ultimate vision.
    - Key Point: Think of consistency as a repetitive signal. Just as intense itching demands the brain's attention, consistent effort demands the Cosmic Brain's response.
    - Belief ensures that opportunities align with your purpose, while action ensures the Cosmic Brain has material to work with.

4. **Be Grateful for the Process (Positive Feedback)**

    - Gratitude amplifies the signal to the Cosmic Brain. By expressing thankfulness for small wins, you create a feedback loop that strengthens your connection to the Cosmic Brain.
    - Example: If you're pursuing a new career, celebrate every interview or skill you gain along the way. Gratitude reinforces that the Cosmic Brain's efforts are valued, encouraging further action in your favor.

Why Action is Non-Negotiable

While the Law of Attraction emphasizes belief, the **Cosmic Brain** insists that **action fuels the process.**

- **Analogy of Itching:**

  An itch triggers the brain only when the cells consistently signal irritation. If the signal is weak, the brain ignores it. Similarly, the Cosmic Brain responds only to consistent and clear actions toward your goal.

- This explains why successful individuals achieve their dreams. It's not solely their belief but the **steps they've taken**—overcoming obstacles, learning new skills, and persevering despite challenges—that sends a continuous signal to the Cosmic Brain.

Why the Cosmic Brain Responds to Intensity and Clarity

The Cosmic Brain operates on the **intensity of your signal** and the **clarity of your purpose.**

1. **Intensity**: Stronger, consistent efforts yield faster responses.
    - **Example:** If someone is intensely passionate about building a business, they will work tirelessly, sending clear signals. The Cosmic Brain will create opportunities that match this drive.
2. **Clarity**: The Cosmic Brain cannot act on vague desires. Be specific and deliberate about your goals.
    - **Example:** Instead of saying, "I want to be successful," define what success means—financial independence, a specific career, or global recognition.

The Cosmic Brain's Four-Step Model

1. **Desire:** Allow yourself to dream big without doubting its possibility.
2. **First Step:** Begin taking action, even if it's small or imperfect. This initiates the signal.
3. **Consistency & Belief:** Combine persistent effort with faith in your ultimate goal. This strengthens the signal.

4. **Gratitude:** Celebrate progress to reinforce the Cosmic Brain's responses.

Summary: Cosmic Brain Over Law of Attraction

Aspect	**Law of Attraction**	**Cosmic Brain**
Focus	Belief and Manifestation	Desire, Action, Consistency, and Gratitude
Core Steps	Ask, Believe, Receive	Desire, Act, Believe Consistently, Show Gratitude
Action Required?	Optional	Mandatory
Key Mechanism	Belief and energy alignment	Intensity and clarity of consistent signals
Outcome	Sometimes vague or delayed	Practical, actionable opportunities and results

The **Cosmic Brain** doesn't just respond to hopes and wishes; it rewards deliberate, persistent effort combined with a focused mind. By shifting from passive manifestation to active creation, you align yourself with the true mechanics of success.

Desires: The Starting Point

Desires: The Starting Point

Desire is the birthplace of all achievements. Every great invention, innovation, and transformation in history began as a spark of longing in someone's mind. But desire is not just a passive thought; it is the seed that sets the process in motion with the Cosmic Brain.

Understanding What You Truly Want

To harness the power of the Cosmic Brain, the first and most crucial step is understanding what you genuinely want. Desires that stem from your core beliefs and aspirations have a stronger signal and a higher likelihood of engaging the Cosmic Brain effectively.

However, many people struggle with defining their true desires. They are often influenced by societal expectations, peer pressure, or superficial motivations. To connect with the Cosmic Brain, you must strip away these external influences and ask yourself:

- What brings you joy?
- What drives your passion?
- What aligns with your values and vision for your life?

When your desires resonate deeply within you, they generate a powerful signal, setting the foundation for your journey toward achieving them.

The Importance of Clarity and Focus

Clarity is essential when sending signals to the Cosmic Brain. Just as a blurry signal disrupts communication in a radio or phone, vague or conflicting desires dilute the signal you send to the universal force.

Imagine a GPS system. If you input a vague or incorrect destination, it cannot guide you to your goal. Similarly, the Cosmic Brain needs precise directions. You must visualize your desire clearly and hold onto it with unwavering focus.

To enhance clarity and focus:

1. **Define Your Goals**: Break your desires into specific, measurable, and actionable components. For instance, instead of saying, "I want to be successful," define what success means to you.
2. **Visualize the Outcome**: Envision yourself achieving your goal. The more vividly you imagine it, the stronger the connection with the Cosmic Brain.
3. **Avoid Contradictions**: Do not send mixed signals by doubting or second-guessing your desires. Trust the process.

By understanding your true desires and maintaining clarity and focus, you take the first step in activating the Cosmic Brain. It is not enough to wish for something casually; you must desire it with intensity, align your actions with your vision, and trust that the Cosmic Brain will respond.

Effort and Energy: The Signals You Send

Effort and Energy: The Signals You Send

Desires are only the starting point in the journey to achieving your goals. The Cosmic Brain responds to signals, but those signals must be strong, clear, and consistent. Effort and energy are the tools that amplify your message to the universal force, ensuring it feels the urgency and intensity of your request.

Why Action and Intensity Matter

Imagine shouting into an open field: a soft whisper gets lost in the air, but a loud, deliberate yell is heard far and wide. This is how the Cosmic Brain perceives your desires. Casual thoughts or weak intentions are like whispers—they dissipate without impact. It is the intensity of your actions and the energy behind them that give your desires weight.

Action creates momentum. When you take steps toward your goal, no matter how small, you strengthen the signal you send. For example:

- If you desire to build a successful business, research, planning, and execution are the "chemical reactions" that send strong signals to the Cosmic Brain.

- If you wish for better health, adopting habits like exercising or eating mindfully translates your desire into action.

The Cosmic Brain doesn't just respond to what you want—it responds to what you work toward. Consistent effort is proof of your commitment, and it compels the universal force to create opportunities in alignment with your actions.

Aligning Your Thoughts, Emotions, and Actions

To maximize the power of your signal, your thoughts, emotions, and actions must align. Misalignment sends conflicting messages, weakening your connection with the Cosmic Brain.

1. **Thoughts**

   Your thoughts are the blueprint for your reality. Positive, goal-oriented thinking sets the tone for your journey. Doubt, negativity, or fear disrupt the signal and hinder progress. Cultivate a mindset of optimism and possibility.

2. **Emotions**

   Emotions add intensity to your signal. When you deeply feel the desire for your goal, your connection with the Cosmic Brain strengthens. Passion, excitement, and determination amplify the energy you send. Conversely, apathy or indifference weakens it.

   For instance, visualizing your success while feeling the joy and satisfaction it brings makes the Cosmic Brain "listen" more attentively to your signal.

3. **Actions**

   Your actions are the physical manifestation of your commitment. Even small, consistent steps show the Cosmic Brain that you are serious. The more effort you put in, the more your signal intensifies.

Amplifying Your Signal

To ensure the Cosmic Brain hears your call clearly:

- **Be Consistent**: Repeated actions reinforce the signal, much like a radio broadcast that plays continuously rather than sporadically.
- **Maintain Focus**: Stay committed to your goal and avoid distractions that dilute your energy.
- **Balance Energy**: Avoid burnout by balancing intense effort with moments of rest and reflection. This helps sustain your signal over the long term.

When you align your thoughts, emotions, and actions, and consistently channel your energy into meaningful effort, the Cosmic Brain cannot ignore your signal. It begins to work in ways you might not fully understand, orchestrating opportunities and circumstances to bring your goal closer to reality.

Manifestation in Action

Manifestation in Action

The Cosmic Brain does not work in mysterious, miraculous ways—it works in logical, observable patterns. When you send strong, consistent signals through your desires, actions, and emotions, the Cosmic Brain begins to create opportunities that align with your goals. This process of manifestation is not magic but a practical outcome of your effort and alignment with universal forces.

How the Cosmic Brain Creates Opportunities

Opportunities are the Cosmic Brain's response to your signals. Think of it as a feedback loop: your desires and actions act as inputs, and the universe responds with outputs in the form of events, connections, or insights.

Here's how the Cosmic Brain works in response to your signals:

1. **Matching Energy**:

   When you align your thoughts, emotions, and actions with a specific goal, you emit a frequency of energy. The Cosmic Brain picks up on this energy and starts to resonate with it, aligning circumstances and opportunities with your efforts.

   For example:

- If you aspire to become an artist, consistent practice and networking may lead to a chance meeting with a mentor or an invitation to showcase your work.
- If you're working toward better health, you might discover a new fitness program or meet someone who inspires you to stay consistent.

2. **Synchronicity**:

   The Cosmic Brain often creates what people call "coincidences" or "luck." These moments of synchronicity are the result of your signal drawing relevant opportunities into your path. It's not random—it's your focus and effort shaping reality.

3. **Guiding Your Perception**:

   The Cosmic Brain also tunes your mind to notice opportunities you might have overlooked otherwise. When you are committed to a goal, your awareness sharpens, making you more receptive to ideas, people, or events that align with your desires.

Recognizing Opportunities

The Cosmic Brain delivers opportunities, but they are often subtle or disguised. Success depends on your ability to recognize and act upon them.

- **Be Present**: Pay attention to your environment. Opportunities often appear in unexpected forms, such as a casual conversation or a sudden idea.
- **Stay Open-Minded**: Don't dismiss unconventional paths. The Cosmic Brain may present opportunities that challenge your comfort zone or require you to think creatively.
- **Trust Your Intuition**: Your intuition is often a guide to recognizing opportunities. If something feels right, explore it, even if it doesn't immediately make sense.

Seizing Opportunities

Once you identify an opportunity, taking action is crucial. The Cosmic Brain responds to effort, so passivity can cause you to miss the window of manifestation.

- **Act Quickly**: Hesitation can weaken the signal you've built. When an opportunity aligns with your goal, act decisively.
- **Be Adaptable**: Manifestation rarely happens in a straight line. Be flexible and willing to adjust your plans as new opportunities unfold.
- **Stay Persistent**: Not every opportunity will yield immediate results. Some are stepping stones that lead to greater possibilities.

Example of Manifestation in Action

Imagine you desire financial freedom and have been working diligently toward starting your own business.

- **Sending Signals**: You research your industry, network with professionals, and start developing a business plan.
- **Opportunities Emerge**: Through a chance encounter, you meet an investor interested in your concept, or you come across a grant program that aligns with your vision.
- **Recognizing the Opportunity**: You notice the potential in these events and decide to pursue them, even if it means stepping outside your comfort zone.
- **Seizing the Moment**: You pitch your idea to the investor or apply for the grant, taking decisive action that aligns with your ultimate goal.

Manifestation as a Partnership

Manifestation is a dynamic partnership between you and the Cosmic Brain. It requires your consistent effort and a willingness to embrace the opportunities presented to you. The Cosmic Brain is not a genie granting wishes; it is a force responding to your intensity, focus, and commitment.

When you recognize and seize the opportunities it creates, you activate the full potential of the Cosmic Brain, moving closer to the life you desire

Be Grateful for the Process

Be Grateful for the Process: Amplify the Signal Through Positive Feedback

Gratitude is a powerful tool that enhances your connection to the Cosmic Brain. By consciously expressing thankfulness for even the smallest progress or victories, you create a positive feedback loop. This loop not only sustains your momentum but also signals to the Cosmic Brain that its efforts are acknowledged and appreciated, encouraging it to align even more opportunities in your favor.

Why Gratitude Matters

Gratitude works as an amplifier for your signal to the Cosmic Brain:

1. **Strengthens the Connection**: Regular expressions of gratitude show the Cosmic Brain that you value its responses, reinforcing your alignment with its processes.
2. **Shifts Focus to Positivity**: Gratitude keeps your mindset attuned to progress rather than setbacks, increasing your energy and clarity.

3. **Motivates Continuous Action**: Recognizing small achievements provides the encouragement needed to stay consistent and persistent in your efforts.

Example: Career Progress

Imagine you're working toward a new career. Along the way, you might encounter milestones like:

- Receiving a call-back for an interview.
- Gaining a new skill through a course or mentorship.
- Networking with someone in your desired field.

Each of these is a step forward, even if they don't immediately lead to your ultimate goal. By expressing gratitude for these small wins—through journaling, meditation, or simply acknowledging them—you signal to the Cosmic Brain that its assistance is appreciated and effective. This encourages the alignment of further opportunities, increasing your chances of achieving your ultimate goal.

Cultivating Gratitude Daily

- **Keep a Gratitude Journal**: Write down three things you're thankful for each day, especially those related to your goals.
- **Celebrate Small Wins**: Treat each accomplishment as a victory, no matter how minor it seems.
- **Share Your Thanks**: Express appreciation to others who help or support you along the way.

By embracing gratitude, you not only elevate your personal experience but also strengthen the Cosmic Brain's ability to work with you, turning aspirations into reality.

Nazar

Nazar and the Cosmic Brain: Understanding the Concept of "Evil Eye"

The concept of **Nazar Lagana** (the "evil eye") is a traditional belief prevalent in many cultures. It suggests that someone else's envious or malicious gaze can negatively affect your success, health, or well-being. While this idea often borders on superstition, when interpreted through the framework of the **Cosmic Brain**, it reveals an interesting perspective about the influence of collective desire and intensity.

Two Major Reasons for Failure According to the Cosmic Brain

1. **Faint Signals to the Cosmic Brain**
   - When you fail to consistently work toward your goal or lose faith in the process, the signals you send to the Cosmic Brain weaken.

- A weak signal results in little to no response from the Cosmic Brain. Your efforts become sporadic, and opportunities don't align with your desires.
  - **Example:**
    - Imagine someone starts a fitness journey but skips workouts frequently and doubts their ability to stay consistent. Their lack of effort and belief weakens the signal, and progress slows down or halts altogether.

2. **Nazar Lagana (The Interference of Opposing Desires)**

- The Cosmic Brain responds to intensity and clarity of desire, regardless of the intent behind it. If someone else strongly desires your failure or misfortune with more intensity than your own efforts to succeed, their negative intent can interfere with the cosmic process.
- How It Works:
  - Just as the Cosmic Brain responds to your signals, it also responds to the desires of others. If their focus and intensity are greater than yours, their desires can temporarily override yours.
  - For example, a person wishing intensely for you to fail (whether out of envy or malice) may create stronger ripples in the cosmic field, disrupting your path.

The Cosmic Brain's Neutrality

The Cosmic Brain doesn't differentiate between positive and negative desires; it simply responds to intensity and consistency. It operates on universal principles, much like natural laws such as gravity. This neutrality means that anyone, regardless of their intentions, can influence outcomes if their signals are strong enough.

How to Overcome Nazar and Strengthen Your Connection with the Cosmic Brain

1. **Strengthen Your Signal**
   - The best defense against external interference is a strong, consistent signal to the Cosmic Brain. This means working with unwavering focus, believing in your goals, and maintaining clarity about your desires.
   - Exam**ple:**
     - If someone envies your career success, ensure your actions and belief are so aligned that their interference becomes negligible.
2. **Stay Consistent**
   - Consistency ensures that your connection with the Cosmic Brain remains dominant. Sporadic efforts or doubts weaken your signal, making it easier for external desires to take precedence.
3. **Positive Intent for Others**
   - By wishing success and positivity for others, you reduce the intensity of negative influences around you. Positivity creates an aura of mutual progress, making it harder for negative desires to gain momentum.
   - **Example:**
     - If you notice someone envying you, actively counter it by spreading goodwill or focusing on their strengths.

4. **Shielding Through Clarity and Gratitude**
    - Be clear about your goals and express gratitude for every milestone. Gratitude amplifies your connection with the Cosmic Brain, making it harder for others' desires to disrupt your progress.

A Practical Analogy

Think of the Cosmic Brain as a radio receiver, and your desires as signals. A strong, clear signal gets through without interference, but a weak signal can be drowned out by noise. Someone's negative energy or "Nazar" acts as static, disrupting your channel. To ensure your frequency dominates, you must:

- Turn up your signal strength (consistent effort and belief).
- Minimize noise (negative energy or distractions).

Nazar: A Reminder of Collective Influence

The concept of Nazar serves as a reminder that we live in a connected universe, where the desires and actions of others can influence outcomes. However, it's also a testament to the power of our own efforts and belief. By staying consistent and focused, you can ensure your connection with the Cosmic Brain remains unshaken, overpowering any external interference.

In essence, the Cosmic Brain rewards those who send the clearest, most persistent signals, no matter the challenges or negativity around them.

Redefining Life

Redefining Life, the Universe, and Human Potential

The concept of the Cosmic Brain transforms our understanding of existence by presenting the universe as an interconnected system that responds to desires, effort, and intent. It shifts the narrative from a world governed by blind faith or random chance to one where individuals play an active role in shaping their destiny.

Life

Instead of perceiving life as a series of predetermined events or as governed by an external, divine force, the Cosmic Brain reframes life as a dynamic interaction between personal effort and universal intelligence. Every desire and action contributes to a feedback loop that shapes experiences, empowering individuals to take control of their journey.

The Universe

The Cosmic Brain replaces traditional notions of a deity with a rational, universal intelligence that operates impartially, responding to intensity and consistency. It suggests that the universe is neither chaotic nor biased but follows natural laws that are accessible to all, regardless of belief or background.

Human Potential

The Cosmic Brain emphasizes that every individual has the ability to manifest their desires and achieve extraordinary outcomes. It removes limitations imposed by fate, superstition, or societal constructs, urging individuals to harness their innate power through focused desire, consistent effort, and belief. This philosophy unlocks new levels of creativity, resilience, and achievement, demonstrating that potential is boundless when aligned with universal principles.

By integrating these ideas into daily life, we can move from being passive observers to active participants in the grand design of the universe, redefining what it means to live a fulfilling and purposeful existence.

Call to Action

A Call to Action: Harness the Power of the Cosmic Brain

To anyone feeling lost in their quest for meaning, purpose, or success: this is your invitation to see the world through a new lens. Have you ever wondered why some prayers seem to be answered while others go unheard? Or why manifestations work for some people but not for others? How is it that those who dedicate themselves wholeheartedly to their goals achieve remarkable success, even when the odds seem stacked against them?

The Cosmic Brain offers an illuminating answer. It explains the processes that govern the universe, helping you understand how desires turn into reality, why persistence leads to breakthroughs, and how life can transform in unexpected, almost magical ways.

This philosophy is not about blind faith or mystical rituals. It is about aligning with the natural laws of the universe—a practical, results-driven approach to manifesting your goals. It challenges outdated beliefs, replacing superstition with purpose, and provides you with tools to actively shape your destiny.

No matter where you stand today—whether you're rebuilding after failure, chasing a long-held dream, or simply searching for clarity—this is your opportunity to take charge. The Cosmic Brain responds to intention, focus, and action, creating pathways to fulfillment and success.

This is your call to action. Begin by identifying your true desires. Take that first step, no matter how small, and consistently work toward your goals with faith in the process. The universe is ready to respond; all it needs is your signal.

Empower yourself by embracing this perspective, and become the architect of your own reality. The path to transformation is in your hands—start walking it today.

Exercises to Practise

Exercises and Worksheets: Practical Activities to Align with the Cosmic Brain

To help readers clarify their desires, plan their efforts, and align with the Cosmic Brain, here are several exercises and worksheets designed to facilitate personal growth and manifestation. These activities will guide you in sending clearer, stronger signals to the Cosmic Brain and provide actionable steps to move toward your goals.

Exercise 1: Clarifying Your Desires

Goal: To identify and articulate your true desires, focusing on what you truly want in life.

Instructions:

1. Find a quiet space and take a few moments to relax and breathe deeply.
2. Grab a pen and paper or use a digital document to write down the following:

- **Desire 1:** What is the most important goal or desire you have right now? (e.g., career, health, relationships)
- **Desire 2:** What else do you desire, even if it seems big or impossible? Be specific.
- **Desire 3:** Is there a smaller, more achievable goal related to your larger desires? (e.g., learning a new skill or taking a first step toward a dream)

3. Reflect on why these desires are meaningful to you. What do they represent i n your life? Write down your reflections.

Worksheet Prompt:

- What are the emotions tied to these desires? Why is this important for your growth?
- How do these desires align with your values and purpose?

Exercise 2: The First Step of Action

Goal: To take the first step toward your desired goal, even if it feels small or uncertain.

Instructions:

1. Choose one of the desires you wrote down in the previous exercise.
2. Write down the first concrete action you can take to start working toward that goal. It could be as simple as researching, reaching out to someone, or setting a small milestone.
3. Schedule this action in your calendar and commit to completing it within the next 24-48 hours.

4. Reflect on any fears or doubts that arise as you think about taking this first step. Write about them and challenge them. Why are these fears present? How can you overcome them?

Worksheet Prompt:

- What has stopped you from taking action before, and how can you move past those obstacles this time?
- How does taking this step make you feel about your goal?

Exercise 3: Strengthening Consistency and Focus

Goal: To maintain consistent effort and focus on your desires, sending a strong signal to the Cosmic Brain.

Instructions:

1. Look at the goal you've chosen to work on. Write down the next 5 small actions you can take over the next 7 days that will bring you closer to your goal.
2. Set aside a specific time each day to work on these actions, even if it's just for 10-15 minutes. Consistency is key.
3. Track your progress every day and note how taking these actions make you feel. Write about the impact this consistency is having on your mindset and results.

Worksheet Prompt:

- How can you reinforce your belief in achieving this goal each day?
- What will help you stay motivated even when results aren't immediate?

Exercise 4: Trusting the Process

Goal: To cultivate trust in the Cosmic Brain's ability to create opportunities as you consistently work toward your goal.

Instructions:

1. Reflect on a time in the past when you took action toward a goal, and things worked out in ways you didn't expect. Write about that experience and how the universe created an opportunity you hadn't anticipated.
2. Now, with your current goal in mind, write down any doubts or uncertainties you have about the process. Challenge each of these doubts with an empowering belief or affirmation that you can hold onto.
3. Write down a list of affirmations that help you trust the process and let go of control over how things unfold.

Worksheet Prompt:

- How does it feel to trust in the process, rather than constantly worrying about the "how"?
- What affirmations can you repeat daily to keep your faith strong?

Exercise 5: Gratitude for the Journey

Goal: To cultivate gratitude for every small step, keeping the feedback loop positive and strengthening your connection with the Cosmic Brain.

Instructions:

1. Every evening, take a moment to reflect on the progress you've made toward your goal, no matter how small.
2. Write down three things you're grateful for that day—whether they're big milestones or small steps.
3. Visualize the Cosmic Brain receiving your gratitude, strengthening the universe's response to your efforts.

Worksheet Prompt:

- How does expressing gratitude affect your feelings of progress and success?
- How can you keep a sense of appreciation even when things feel slow or difficult?

Final Worksheet: Aligning with the Cosmic Brain

Goal: To reflect on and integrate everything you've learned in this section to align with the Cosmic Brain.

Instructions:

1. Review all your answers and reflections from the previous exercises.
2. Answer the following questions:
    - What is your ultimate desire, and how does it align with your core values?
    - How are you actively sending a strong, consistent signal to the Cosmic Brain? What actions will you take moving forward?

- How do you trust the Cosmic Brain to find the path to your goal?
- What is your daily routine for reinforcing your desire, action, and belief?

Worksheet Prompt:

- In what ways can you amplify your connection to the Cosmic Brain starting today?
- What new beliefs or habits will you adopt to ensure you stay aligned with your desires and goals?

These exercises are designed to help you manifest your desires and achieve your goals by clarifying your intentions, planning your actions, and aligning with the Cosmic Brain's response. By completing them, you'll build the foundation for consistent, purposeful effort toward the life you want to create.

Connect with Me

I believe in fostering a community of like-minded individuals who are eager to explore new ideas, challenge old beliefs, and grow together. If this book has sparked your curiosity, or if you'd like to continue the conversation about the Cosmic Brain, spirituality, and personal growth, feel free to connect with me on social media.

You can find me at:

Instagram: @the_illusion_breaker

Thank you for taking the time to read my work. Let's continue this journey of exploration and growth together!

www.ingramcontent.com/pod-product-compliance
Lightning Source LLC
LaVergne TN
LVHW091112150826
845673LV00002B/794

* 9 7 9 8 8 9 6 9 9 4 7 8 7 *